CELEBRATING
DÍA DE LOS MUERTOS

CELEBRATING

DÍA DE LOS MUERTOS

History, Traditions, and Activities
A HOLIDAY BOOK FOR KIDS

Melanie Stuart-Campbell

Illustrations by Javiera Mac-lean

ROCKRIDGE
PRESS

First Rockridge Press hardcover edition 2022

Originally published in trade paperback by Rockridge Press 2021

Rockridge Press and the Rockridge Press logo are trademarks or registered trademarks
of Callisto Media Inc. and/or its affiliates in the United States and other countries and
may not be used without written permission.

For general information on our other products and services, please contact our
Customer Care Department within the United States at (866) 744-2665, or outside
 the United States at (510) 253-0500.

Hardcover ISBN: 979-8-88650-447-7 | Paperback ISBN: 978-1-64876-362-5
eBook ISBN: 978-1-64876-363-2

Manufactured in the United States of America

Series Designer: Elizabeth Zuhl
Interior and Cover Designer: Jane Archer
Art Producer: Sara Feinstein
Editor: Alyson Penn
Production Editor: Rachel Taenzler
Production Manager: Holly Haydash

Illustrations © 2021 Javiera Mac-lean

10 9 8 7 6 5 4 3 2 1 0

For all the spirits, both living and not,
who help guide us on our paths—in
particular my mother, my grandparents,
and Alba, the South American Street Dog

CONTENTS

gifts to the spirits of those they love. It is a beautiful way for families to keep the memories of their loved ones alive.

WHAT IS DÍA DE LOS MUERTOS?

Día de los Muertos is Spanish for "Day of the Dead." This holiday began in Mexico, but there are similar celebrations in many parts of the world. People who celebrate Día de los Muertos believe that the souls of their loved ones who have passed away will come back to visit them. It is a happy time when family and close friends, living and in spirit, are believed to reunite and enjoy music, gifts, and food together.

The **festivities** happen over two days every year—November 1 and 2—and are full of color and joy. People participate in parades and parties, dress in skeleton costumes, sing and dance, and give

HISTORY AND FOLKLORE

The traditions of Día de los Muertos go back almost 3,000 years! Some of the **ancestors**, or older relatives, of the Mexican people were the Aztecs. The Aztecs believed there were many gods, including the gods of the dead. The Aztecs called the god of the dead Mictlantecuhtli (pronounced Mict-lahn-te-cuut-li). They pictured him as a smiling skeleton. His wife was Mictecacíhuatl (pronounced Meek-teka-see-waht), Lady of the Dead. For the Aztecs, death was a happy event. It meant that a person's spirit, no longer trapped in a body, would get to move on to a **paradise**.

Every summer, the Aztecs would celebrate death with a festival. They would use skull and skeleton **symbols** as a way to celebrate their belief that a person's soul lives on even after the body dies. Over time, that summer festival was moved to November. Today, it is known as Día de los Muertos. You will see many skulls and skeletons as part of the celebrations.

A CELEBRATION OF CULTURES

About 500 years ago, people from Spain **colonized** Mexico, making it a part of their country. These Spanish people were Catholics. They believed in only one God and the teachings of Jesus Christ. This was very different from the Aztecs, who believed in many gods.

Catholics in Spain celebrated **All Saints' Day** and **All Souls' Day** on November 1 and 2. These holidays also remembered people who had died. After some time, the Aztec beliefs and the Christian beliefs were combined. Some Día de los Muertos symbols and practices come from Christian beliefs, such as crosses and pictures of **saints**. The skull, called *calavera* in Spanish, and the skeleton, called *calaca* in Spanish, are symbols that come from the Aztecs.

Día de los Muertos is a time of great pride when Mexicans remember their loved ones and the history of their beautiful country.

WHEN SOULS REUNITE

During the two days of Día de los Muertos, families gather both at home and at the cemetery to share food and drinks with one another and with the spirits of those they love. Families may pray or sit quietly by the

The Aztecs' big festival to remember their dead loved ones lasted around 20 days and was held in late July and early August.

grave. Some people play guitars or listen to music and share fun stories of their dead loved ones. Sometimes fireworks are set off to help light the path "home" for the spirits. It is also common to read the Bible or to attend a **mass**, which is a religious service at church. More than anything, people feel as if the worlds of the living and the dead come together in celebration. They celebrate the love they have for one another, forever and always.

PREPARATION

Families spend a lot of time preparing for Día de los Muertos. They set up special spaces to welcome the souls of their loved ones home. They make the souls' favorite foods and drinks. Families may also decorate their homes and streets with colorful banners, which are made of tissue paper and have designs cut out of them.

OFRENDAS

An **ofrenda**, or **altar**, is an important part of Día de los Muertos celebrations. Unlike most altars, though, it is for remembering, not worshipping. Found in homes and cemeteries, the *ofrenda* is an entryway for spirits to meet up with their living loved ones.

Ofrendas are not only placed in people's homes or in cemeteries but also can be found in schools, offices, and other public spaces.

Ofrendas for Día de los Muertos are always colorful and welcoming. They are often created on a raised surface and may even have different levels. Each *ofrenda* tells something about the loved one who died. It displays their photo and is usually decorated with candles, food, and colorful marigold flowers. The scent and gold color of the marigolds are believed to help guide the spirit home (sometimes the flowers are even made of paper). An **incense** called *copal* may be burned near the altar so its sweet smell will also help the spirit find their way home. You may even see a welcome mat placed before the altar. A ***papel picado***, a colorful paper banner, is sometimes used to decorate the *ofrenda*. The *ofrendas* are taken down during the evening of November 2.

Pets might also be remembered on the *ofrenda*. People place photos of their dogs or cats plus their favorite treats on the altar.

HOW TO MAKE AN OFRENDA

Ofrenda means "offering" in Spanish. There are no real rules for what to include in an *ofrenda*. An *ofrenda* simply needs to reflect the person being welcomed and could include some of the following things:

- **Photos** to celebrate what the loved one looked like in life.

- **Food and drink** to satisfy the hungry and thirsty spirit who has traveled to see their family.

- A **bowl of water, bar of soap, towel, and mirror** to help the spirit clean up after their journey.

- **Personal belongings**, such as a favorite toy, doll, piece of jewelry, or instrument, to please the spirit and help them find their way back home.

- **Sugar skulls** (see page 30) to represent the person who has passed away and is receiving the offerings.

- **Religious symbols** to help mark the holiday if the family is Catholic.

A YUMMY HOLIDAY!

Food and drink are an important part of many celebrations, and Día de los Muertos is no different. Not only do people prepare and eat delicious food and drinks during this holiday, but they also leave some treats on the *ofrendas*.

You may be thinking, *Spirits don't eat or drink*, but some people do believe that the souls are able to taste during these days. Here are a few examples of the foods enjoyed during Día de los Muertos:

» Hot chocolate or **atole**, which is a hot corn-based beverage.

» **Pan de muerto**, which means "bread of the dead." It is a soft sweet bread shaped like a bun with bone-like designs on top.

» **Tamales**, which are corn dough parcels filled with meat, cheese, and spices and wrapped in corn husks.

» **Calaveritas de azúcar** are small decorated sugar skulls offered to the souls of children.

Calaveritas de azúcar, or sugar skulls, are made of sugar, but you do not want to eat them. Many are made with colored foil, feathers, and beads, which are not **edible**, or good to eat.

A FESTIVE CEMETERY

It is believed that the grave is the first place the spirits visit each year.

To prepare for this great event, families spend a lot of time cleaning and decorating the grave sites. They pull weeds and make sure that the grass is cut. If any trash is around, they put it in the garbage. They also wash the tombstone so it is perfectly clean.

Many people also place a **corona**, or wreath, of flowers on the grave. These *coronas* can be made of real flowers, tissue paper flowers, or both. Some families sleep beside the cleaned and decorated grave for a night or two—it is like a slumber party!

HOW TO CELEBRATE

Día de los Muertos is a celebration of life and death. Some people may confuse it with Halloween because it is celebrated around the same time, but the two holidays are very different. During Día de los Muertos, people come together to celebrate and remember their dead family and friends. They feel joyful as they tell stories and honor the memory of their loved ones. It's not scary or sad at all. It's colorful and fun. Everyone has a wonderful time.

THE DAY OF THE CHILDREN

On the morning of November 1, church bells ring—a signal that all the spirits and the living should go to the cemetery. This day is for remembering and celebrating the souls of children, the young **angelitos**, or "little angels," who have passed on. Families may place breakfast, chocolate, flowers, or balloons on the *ofrenda* for the young spirits. They may also place a sugar skull with the child's name near the grave.

Around noon, the spirits of the children are believed to depart until the next year. Then families get ready to welcome the spirits of the adults. It is common for people to dress up as skeletons as they celebrate both life and death. One of the most popular costumes is a woman skeleton wearing a big fancy hat. The festivities last until the end of the day on November 2.

SHARING STORIES

Día de los Muertos is a happy time for family members to share stories and memories about loved ones who have died. By talking about their ancestors, friends and relatives are kept "alive" in memory, which makes family bonds stronger. When you hear stories, year after year, about a great-grandparent, or aunt, or cousin who died before you were born, you feel like you know them.

The stories that are shared are mainly funny ones. Because it is a festive time, the conversation is about good things. You might also hear about special talents of the dead ancestors, like how your uncle was a great singer or what a fantastic cook your grandmother was. As these stories get passed down from **generation** to generation, the loved ones are always remembered.

In some places, people call November 1 *Día de los Inocentes*, or Day of the Innocents, when they remember and celebrate the spirits of children.

PARADES

During Día de los Muertos you will see many skeleton costumes and skull face paintings at parades. The most popular *calavera* is called La Catrina. La Catrina first appeared as a cartoon skeleton wearing fancy clothes in a Mexican newspaper in 1913. She wears nice clothes and an elegant hat. When people dress like La Catrina, they remind us that death happens to everybody, no matter how much money you have or where you are from.

What else might you see at these parades? In addition to La Catrina costumes and other *calaveras*, you will see a lot of people playing music. You will hear drums, guitars, trumpets, and plenty of traditional Mexican folk music called **mariachi**.

La Catrina is a famous female skeleton whose image appears on a mural in Mexico City. The mural was painted by one of Mexico's most popular artists, Diego Rivera.

LA MÚSICA

Music is an important part of many celebrations, including Día de los Muertos. People play guitars and other instruments, and there is also lots of singing. The lively music can be heard in many places, such as in cemeteries, in homes, and on the streets.

Some families hire a mariachi band to play traditional folk music. Mariachi bands usually have several band members playing many instruments. The bands play at cemeteries, parades, and other parties to welcome back the spirits. The most popular song you will hear is "La Llorona," or "The Crying Woman," which first became popular in Mexico in 1941. Another song you may hear is "Calaverita," or "The Little Skull," which was written by a band from California in 2015. Often the lyrics are centered on celebrating life, which is what these special days are all about.

AROUND THE WORLD

Día de los Muertos started in Mexico, but similar celebrations happen in other parts of the world. Because people **migrate**, or move from one place to another, you may see traditions like those in Mexico celebrated in other countries. When people move from one country to another, they often bring some of their traditions with them.

Just like the Spaniards brought their beliefs of All Saints' Day and All Souls' Day to Mexico, they also took those beliefs to other places that they colonized, such as countries in Central America, South America, and the **Caribbean**, and to the Philippines (in Asia). Because of this migration and the sharing of traditions, people in different places celebrate their dead loved ones in similar ways.

CELEBRATIONS IN MEXICO

Mexico is where Día de los Muertos began, and it is the country that celebrates it with the most enthusiasm.

A very popular parade is held in Mexico City every year, and thousands of people travel to watch it. It is the biggest Day of the Dead parade in the world. There are colorful floats, live music, and many people wearing elaborate skeleton costumes.

In Michoacán, Mexico, there is a popular dance called La Danza de los Viejitos, or The Dance of the Old Men. Both adults and children dress up like old men and walk around bent over, and then suddenly jump up and start dancing wildly.

In Oaxaca, Mexico, they have street parties called *calendas* where you will see giant puppets on **stilts**. There are also many face-painting stands set up around town, ready to paint people's faces to look like skulls.

Many **tourists** come to see the celebrations that take place on a small island called Janitzio in the western part of Mexico. The local people celebrate at the cemetery throughout the two nights.

CELEBRATIONS BEYOND MEXICO

People in other countries also celebrate these two days in some interesting ways.

On November 1, Guatemalans host the Festival de Barriletes Gigantes, or Giant Kite Festival. Thousands of people get together to fly huge, colorful kites that have been painted by hand. It is believed that the kites pass messages to and from dead loved ones.

In the Philippines, families get together for Undás, or All Saints' Day and All Souls' Day. This celebration is similar to Día de los Muertos, although you won't see

any skulls. It is common for families to travel long distances to see relatives whom they may not have seen since the last year's Undás. People also make altars and bring food to the cemeteries on this important national holiday.

In Spain and in most countries in South America, it is more common to celebrate Día de Todos los Santos (All Saints' Day) on November 1, and Día de los Difuntos (Day of the Deceased or All Souls' Day) on November 2.

In some countries, Roman Catholics and Christians celebrate All Saints' Day as a national holiday. On these days, people remember the many saints and attend mass at church. On All Souls' Day, some families bring flowers to cemeteries and visit the graves of their dead loved ones, similar to Memorial Day in the United States.

In El Salvador, La Calabiuza, or The Feast of the Dead, is held on the night of November 1. People celebrate their lost loved ones with music and dancing in the middle of town.

CULTURE CORNER

Día de los Muertos is a special occasion when people get to participate in crafts, activities, and making recipes. Try these with family or friends to honor the holiday in your home.

PAPEL PICADO

A *papel picado* is a tissue paper banner with colorful cutout patterns—skeleton figures or flower designs are especially common during Día de Los Muertos. Paper is used because it is light and can move easily, letting families know when the spirts have arrived. You can find many templates online to make cutting out the shapes easier.

Scissors

4 sheets of different-colored tissue paper (1 of each color)

Pencil or marker

String or yarn

Clear tape

1. Using the scissors, cut each of the 4 colored pieces of paper into a 9-by-6-inch rectangle.

2. Place the rectangles on a clean, flat work surface. Fold each rectangle in half.

3. Using a pencil or marker, draw designs along all four edges of each folded rectangle. Leave a space between each shape.

4. Using the scissors, cut out each shape you drew. Unfold the papers to see your designs.

5. Arrange the string or yarn in a straight line. Evenly space each piece of paper along the string, overlapping the edges slightly. Then fold it over the string, and tape it down.

6. Tie your colorful banner somewhere in your house or yard.

PAN DE MUERTO, OR BREAD OF THE DEAD

Pan de muerto is a very popular Mexican sweet bread. It is also the most common food you will find on an *ofrenda* during Día de los Muertos. The round shape symbolizes the circle of life, and the shapes on top represent bones. When you make *pan de muerto*, ask an adult to help you with the oven.

Makes: 1 loaf
Prep time: 1 hour and 15 minutes, plus 1 hour and 30 minutes to 2 hours and 30 minutes to rise
Cook time: 40 minutes

¼ **cup milk**

¼ **cup butter, melted**

¼ **cup warm water**

3 cups all-purpose flour, divided, plus more for dusting

1¼ teaspoons active dry yeast

¼ **cup granulated sugar**

2 teaspoons whole anise seeds

½ **teaspoon salt**

2 large eggs, at room temperature, beaten

Nonstick cooking spray

1 egg white

1 tablespoon water

2 tablespoons colored sugar (your choice of color)

1. In a medium saucepan over medium-low heat, heat the milk and butter. Stir occasionally, just until the butter is melted. Remove the pan from the heat. Stir in the warm water. Set aside.

26

2. In a large bowl, place 1 cup of flour. Add the yeast, sugar, anise seeds, and salt. Mix to combine. Then add the warm milk mixture (from step 1) and the eggs. Mix well. Add ½ cup of flour. Mix until combined. Continue adding more flour, ½ cup at a time, and stir until the mixture comes together to form a soft dough.

3. Turn the dough out of the bowl onto a clean, lightly floured work surface. Using your hands, knead the dough until it feels smooth but still a bit sticky.

4. Lightly grease a large bowl with cooking spray. Place the dough in the greased bowl. Cover the bowl with plastic wrap. Set the covered bowl aside in a warm place and let it rise until it doubles in size, 1 to 2 hours.

5. Lightly grease a baking sheet with cooking spray and set it aside.

6. Once the dough has doubled in size, turn it out onto a lightly floured surface. Knead it again for about 3 minutes.

7. Tear off a piece of dough about the size of your fist. Set it aside. Shape the remaining dough into a smooth round loaf. Place the loaf on your prepared baking sheet.

8. Take the dough you set aside and separate it into 9 equal-size balls. You will use these balls to decorate your loaf. Place one ball on the center top of the loaf. Arrange the other balls around it to make an X shape. Cover the loaf with a clean kitchen towel. Set the pan aside in a warm place until the loaf doubles in size, about 30 minutes.

9. About 15 minutes before you are ready to bake the bread, preheat your oven to 350°F.

10. In a small bowl, whisk together the egg white and 1 tablespoon of water. Using a pastry brush, cover the loaf with the egg white and water mixture. Sprinkle the colored sugar all over the top of the loaf.

11. Carefully place your pan in the preheated oven. Bake your loaf until the top is lightly golden brown, about 40 minutes. Remove the pan from the oven. Transfer your baked *pan de muerto* to a wire rack to cool for about 10 minutes. Enjoy!

FLOR DE MUERTO

With their strong scent and gold color, marigolds are believed to help guide spirits back to their *ofrendas* or graves on Día de Los Muertos. Try making these paper marigolds. You can display them in a vase or tie them on a string to make a festive garland.

---

1 orange cocktail napkin   **1 green pipe cleaner**

Scissors

1. Open up the napkin and place it flat on a clean work surface.

2. Using the scissors, cut along the creases to make four separate squares.

3. Stack the squares on top of one another. Then fold up one edge of your stack about ¼ inch. Continue folding the paper into an accordion fan.

4. Take one end of the pipe cleaner and twist it very tightly around the center of your fan to form your flower's stem.

5. Using the scissors, carefully trim the edges off each end of your fan so the corners are rounded.

6. Hold your fan with the stem pointing straight down. Then, starting with one side of your fan, gently pull up one layer of paper. Continue to separate the remaining three layers of paper, one by one, to form the petals. Repeat on the other side of the flower.

7. Once all the layers are separated, fluff and arrange them to look like a marigold.

MARSHMALLOW SUGAR SKULL POPS

During Día de los Muertos, *calaveritas de azúcar*, or sugar skulls, decorate the altars and graves. It is believed that the visiting spirits are happy to be greeted with a sugary treat. You can make your own safe-to-eat *calaveritas de azúcar* using marshmallows and edible ink markers.

Choose marshmallows that have a clean, smooth shape for the best result. Place your sugar skull pops in a mug stuffed with shredded paper to display them—that is, if you don't eat them first!

Colored edible ink markers

4 jumbo marshmallows

4 lollipop or candy sticks or straws

1. Using a black edible ink marker, draw eyes, a nose, and a mouth on each marshmallow. Use the other colored edible ink markers to have fun decorating the rest of the skull with different designs.

2. When you have completed your designs, insert a stick or straw into the bottom of each marshmallow to use as a handle.

Tip: You can find edible ink markers at craft and baking supply stores.

PIN THE HAT ON THE CALACA (SKELETON)

This game is similar to Pin the Tail on the Donkey. With a blindfold on, the player is spun around and becomes dizzy, and then tries to find the skeleton's head to place the hat on it.

Markers

White poster board

Sheet of white card stock

Scissors

Glue (optional)

Sequins and pom-poms (optional)

Sticky tack

Blindfold

HOW TO PREPARE

1. Using the markers, draw a skeleton on the poster board. Set it aside.

2. Draw a big fancy hat on the card stock. Using the scissors, carefully cut it out.

3. Using the markers, color in the hat. You can glue on sequins and pom-poms to decorate it if you like.

4. Place sticky tack on the back of the hat.

HOW TO PLAY

1. Blindfold the person playing. Have them stand about 3 feet in front of the *calaca*.

2. Place the hat in their hands, with the sticky tack side facing away from them, and spin them around 3 times. When you say, "Go!" it's their job to try to place the hat on the skeleton.

continued ➤

PIN THE HAT ON THE CALACA continued

3. As the person is trying to find the skeleton's head, chant this slowly: "You are looking for the head to place the hat upon the dead. Count to five, your time will end. Then pass the hat to your friend. 1-2-3-4-5!"

4. Repeat this with each player until somebody gets the hat on top of the skeleton's head. The winner gets one of your Marshmallow Sugar Skull Pops (see page 30) or a prize of your choosing.

Variation: Instead of drawing the skeleton on the poster board, you can find skeleton outlines online, print them out, cut them out, and glue them to the poster board.

LEARN TO SAY IT!

Here are some common phrases that people say on Día de los Muertos.

Es Día de los Muertos.
IT'S DAY OF THE DEAD.

Qué rico es el pan de muerto.
THE BREAD OF THE DEAD IS VERY TASTY.

¿Me da una calaverita de azúcar?
MAY I HAVE A SUGAR SKULL CANDY?

La ofrenda es muy bonita.
THE ALTAR IS VERY BEAUTIFUL.

Mi cara está pintada como una calavera.
MY FACE IS PAINTED LIKE A SKULL.

GLOSSARY

All Saints' Day: A day to honor all the saints, celebrated by Christians on November 1

All Souls' Day: A day to remember those who have passed away, observed by Christians on November 2

altar: A raised structure, such as a table, with objects on top to honor someone; see *ofrenda*

ancestor: A relative or someone from whom you are descended

angelitos: Spanish for "little angels," referring to the spirits of children who have died

atole: A traditional corn-based hot drink from Mexico and Central America

calaca: Spanish for "skeleton"

calavera: Spanish for "skull"

calaveritas de azúcar: Small sugar skulls used to decorate altars and sometimes for eating

Caribbean: The body of water between North and South America that has several islands

ntry takes control of

aced on the grave sides of

los Muertos

panish for "Day of the Dead"

hat you can eat

rations or parties

People who are living at the same time

close in age

ense: A substance that makes a sweet scent

when burned

mariachi: A group of Mexican folk musicians who

sing and play many instruments. Mariachi is also the

name of the music they play

mass: A special church service for Catholics

migrate: When a person moves from one region of

the world to another

ofrenda: Spanish for "altar" or "offering," which is

something to give

pan de muerto: A special sweet bread with bone-like

designs on top, mainly enjoyed during Día de

los Muertos

pel picado: Paper or tissue banners with designs cut out that are used as decorations Mexican celebrations

paradise: A heaven-like place where people's sp go after they die

saint: A holy and godly person who cares greatly for others

stilts: Poles that attach to your feet to make you stand very tall

symbol: An object or mark that stands for an idea

tamales: A traditional Mexican dish made of dough and steamed in a corn husk, stuffed with meat, cheese, and spices

tourist: Someone who travels for fun

RESOURCES

BOOKS

Greenfield Thong, Roseanne. *Día de los Muertos.* Park Ridge, IL: Albert Whitman & Company, 2015.

Johnston, Tony, and Jeanette Winter. *Day of the Dead.* Boston: HMH Books for Young Readers, 2000.

MOVIE

Coco: Directed by Adrian Molina and Lee Unkrich, Walt Disney Studios Motion Pictures, 2017.

WEBSITES

Day of the Dead Coloring Pages: BestColoring Pagesforkids.com/free-printable-day-dead-coloring -pages.html.

Día de los Muertos Flash Cards: azcentral.com/story /entertainment/holidays/day-of-the-dead/2014/09/25 /dia-de-los-muertos-flash-cards/16232843.

National Geographic: "Top 10 Things to Know about the Day of the Dead." NationalGeographic.com/travel /destinations/north-america/mexico/top-ten-day-of -dead-mexico.

ABOUT THE AUTHOR

 **Melanie Stuart-Campbell** is also the author of *Alba, the South American Street Dog, Learn Spanish with Pictures*, and *A Spanish Workbook for Kids*. She is an instructional specialist and advocate for the Kansas Migrant Education Program, working with many people who celebrate Día de los Muertos. She also teaches online Spanish classes to kids on the website Outschool. Melanie has been a teacher in Kansas, New York City, Ecuador, and the Republic of Congo. She lives in Kansas with her husband and two children, and serves on her local school board. You can see her other books on her website AlbasSpanishTales.com.

ABOUT THE ILLUSTRATOR

Illustrator **Javiera Mac-lean** has written and illustrated two children's books, *The Cloud in the Window* and *Folding Adventure*, both published by Bibliográfica Internacional, as well as other books related to child psychology. She has also illustrated for multinational companies and magazines in the United States, Chile, and Spain. In 2017 she studied illustration at the EINA School. You can see her work on Instagram @Javiera-Maclean.